Competitive Strateg

Winning Strategies

The Top 100 Best Strategies For Peak Performance During Competitions

By Ace McCloud
Copyright © 2015

Disclaimer

The information provided in this book is designed to provide helpful information on the subjects discussed. This book is not meant to be used, nor should it be used, to diagnose or treat any medical condition. For diagnosis or treatment of any medical problem, consult your own physician. The publisher and author are not responsible for any specific health or allergy needs that may require medical supervision and are not liable for any damages or negative consequences from any treatment, action, application or preparation, to any person reading or following the information in this book. Any references included are provided for informational purposes only. Readers should be aware that any websites or links listed in this book may change.

Table of Contents

DEDICATED TO THOSE WHO ARE PLAYING THE GAME OF LIFE TO

WIN

KEEP ON PUSHING AND NEVER GIVE UP!

Ace McCloud

Be sure to check out my website for all my Books and Audio books.

www.AcesEbooks.com

Introduction

I want to thank you and congratulate you for buying the book, "Competitive Strategy: Winning Strategies- The Top 100 Best Strategies for Peak Performance During Competitions."

No matter where you are in life or what you're doing, you're always going to have competition. To many, competition is a negative word. In their mind, competition equals trash talk and trying to humiliate the opponent. However, for the most part, competition in business occurs when two companies have products that are similar but slightly different. For example, Facebook and Myspace were once competitors; they are both social media websites but with different features. Burger King and Wendy's are competitors – two fast food restaurants that serve up burgers but with different toppings. Competition doesn't have to be between businesses – it can be between two or more people. If you're running a race, the other racers are your competition. If you're fighting for a promotion, the other people in your office are your competitors. Each person has unique qualities that they excel at.

Life, in many ways, is all about winning. Today's society can be a cutthroat world and the reality is that you must often fight for the things you want. In order to succeed and accomplish your dreams and goals, it helps to harness your competitive nature. While hard work pays off, you will succeed much more often if you are utilizing a strategy along with hard work to get your desired result. It also helps if you can stoke your inner drive and develop a burning passion to win and succeed! Your passion to win must be strong enough that you are willing to pay the necessary price to reach your goal. That's where competitive advantage comes in. With the right mindset and the right strategies you can acquire the upper edge when it comes to winning and accomplishing your goals.

Without applying winning strategies to your goals, you risk living a mediocre life and you are much more likely to be frustrated and angry. Many people make the mistake of not preparing for the goals that they want to achieve. For example, they may think of getting a promotion like this: "I hope they recognize my talent and reward my hard work." However, that mindset is a bad strategy that will take you much longer to get the desired results. Being unprepared often prevents you from doing what you need to do in order to win. When you don't feel like you are winning in your life, you are more likely to feel unmotivated, sad or depressed.

However, when you *do* prepare yourself to compete, you will often find yourself in a much better position to win. There is no better feeling in the world than winning! When you are a winner, you are more likely to feel energized, happy and productive. One of the best and easiest ways to prepare yourself for success in life is to discover how to implement some of the world's best competitive strategies towards your goals.

This book contains proven steps and peak performance strategies that you can use to stoke your competitive desires in order to help you to achieve your desired results. A winning strategy has different components, depending on your goal and what you are trying to accomplish. It requires building healthy habits, developing strong self-discipline, feeding your motivation, making a plan and much more. Within this book, you will discover how to bring out the best in yourself so that you can stay on top of your game and compete at a much higher level to achieve your desired levels of success!

Chapter 1: Building A Powerful Attitude

When it comes to achieving any goal in life, attitude must be a key part of your winning strategy. Starting off with the wrong attitude is a surefire way to kill any chance of success. Starting off with the *right* attitude allows you to set yourself up for success as early as possible. Many people develop their general attitude during childhood. Their attitude is often shaped by life-changing events, both good and bad. However, with enough willpower, it is possible to transform a negative attitude into a positive one.

Many famous people in history made it big, not because of their education, wealth or social status, but because of their attitude. There are three components to your attitude: emotion, cognition and behavior. Your attitude can color your emotions and impact your opinions. Your attitude can also affect how you think about things and what you believe about yourself and others; this is known as cognition. It can also influence your behavior, meaning that your attitude often drives – or inhibits – your actions.

The first step in your winning strategy is to set your attitude to "good." Although it may be challenging at first, it is an amazing feeling to transform a bad attitude into a positive one. This chapter will help you do this in order to reach your goals.

Positive Affirmations (as featured in my book on Attitude)

Affirmations are words and sentences that you say to yourself in order to get your mind in the right frame of mind to accomplish your desired goals. Affirmations build confidence within your positive attitude. If you tell yourself you can do something or that you are good at something, you are more likely to be able to complete the task. Some examples of positive affirmations are:

• I deserve to be happy.

• I am smart enough and organized enough to get a good paying job.

• I am worthy of love.

• I see the good in all people and situations.

• I love my life.

• I am generous, giving and caring every day of my life.

• I act quickly and decisively.

• I am going to be a winner today.

- I will improve myself every day by following good habits, eating healthy and promoting good relationships in my life.

- I am super strong, healthy, wealthy and wise.

- I am super creative and perform flawlessly.

- I love to compete and give my best each and every time.

Here is an exercise for you to try right now:

- Think about the goal that you are trying to achieve. This will be the first step in creating your winning strategy. I want you to think of **three** positive affirmations you can speak out loud or to yourself in your mind. You can pick from the aforementioned list or you can create some that are personal and more relative to your goal. Say these affirmations out loud or in your head wherever you are. Repeat these affirmations while you're in the shower, brushing your teeth, driving to work, having lunch, cleaning your house, walking, etc. Continue practicing these affirmations until you start feeling them from within.

A Morning/Evening Ritual (as featured in my book on <u>Attitude</u>)

Many people find their lives are enhanced by performing a morning and/or evening ritual. A ritual is a certain succession of actions that help reinforce beliefs and attitudes.

What kind of attitude would you foster if every morning you woke up, turned off the alarm and grumbled when you had to get up? Surprisingly, or maybe not so surprisingly, this is what most people do. They would rather dream the day away in bed than meet it headlong in order to reach and actually hold their dreams. How much better would their day go if they woke up with a smile, ready to take on whatever came?

Rituals do not have to take much time. Waking up 15 to 20 minutes early is all you really need unless you want to incorporate physical exercise, a shower and getting ready. I personally started doing my new morning routine several months ago and I have noticed a huge difference in not only my productivity, but my overall energy levels and happiness as well! To go along with that, my attitude has been great!

Check out the following suggestions on how to foster a positive attitude with a morning ritual:

1. As soon as consciousness seeps in; smile. Stretch those lips in an upward position to start your day off right.

2. Breathe deeply. This will get your blood circulating and will start sending blood to all those muscles that have been relaxed all night long. Lie on your back and place your hands on your stomach, under your ribs. Breathe in slowly and deliberately, preferably through your nose. As you breathe in, your stomach should rise up a bit. Your shoulders should not rise. Hold the breath and breathe out through your lips like you are blowing out a candle. Do this as slowly as you can. While you breathe out, your stomach will sink down again. Take about 5 good breaths, thinking only about breathing in and out.

3. Once you've really started breathing, think of three or four things you are most grateful for. It can be your family, your job, your pet or anything else. This should only take a few moments, but take the time to fully feel the gratitude.

4. Breathe in and out quickly about 10 times. This should clear your head and get you ready to start moving.

5. Stretch your muscles starting at your neck and moving down to your shoulders, your arms, your hands, your back and chest, your hips, your stomach, your thighs, your legs and your feet. If you need to sit up to do this, do so. Once you are comfortable with this you will want to use your stretching time to focus on a single goal you wish to achieve. After you have

stretched all muscle groups, set your thoughts aside and get out of bed.

6. Go to the kitchen and drink a full glass of water. You can then exercise if you wish or start the shower. The water will get your digestive system working and will help flush out any toxins that built up in your body overnight.

7. While in the shower, start your litany of positive affirmations. These are phrases that describe you accomplishing a goal or just make you feel good. Repeating positive affirmations is a method that many peak performers do on a regular basis. If you keep saying it, you are affirming it and you will eventually believe it.

You can also add an affirmation stage to your morning ritual. During this time you will state your goals as affirmations. I would affirm being a successful writer who can live off the money I make from writing. A business person might affirm becoming president of their company in five years. A teacher may affirm that he or she will reach the students in class so that they learn and are successful. Take a few more breaths and go out there to meet the day with a smile on your face and bounce in your step.

Bonus Ideas for Your Morning Ritual

1. Do not check your email as soon as you wake up in the morning! If you ignore your email for the first 30 minutes of your day and do your morning ritual first, statistics show that you are over 30% more likely to be more productive during the day.

2. Read for fifteen minutes from a self-development book or a similarly uplifting source of information.

3. Listen to favorite music while stretching or doing yoga for 20 minutes or so.

4. Review all of your goals and then visualize yourself doing and accomplishing them with enthusiasm!

5. Plan to do the most important things first in the day and then work on everything else after that.

6. Eat a nutritious meal early in the day. One of my favorites is organic baby spinach and a banana mixed in my Nutribullet blender to make a delicious and energizing smoothie.

Your evening ritual, should you choose to follow one, should focus on calming the body and mind in order to ready it for sleep while fostering a positive attitude. Here are a few steps you can follow to perform an evening ritual:

1. Do some deep breathing. Deep breathing does waken the body, but it also induces relaxation. Lie in

the bed and slowly breathe in and out, as you did in the morning. Do this five to six times, concentrating only on the breaths you are taking. Empty the mind of everything else.

2. Think about the day that just ended as you set your alarm for tomorrow. Evaluate your progress toward goals and think of three things you did during that day that fulfilled your morning affirmations.

3. If you pray, say your evening prayers. If you do not pray, reinforce some of your favorite affirmations.

4. Write in a journal about all you got accomplished for the day and what you would like to get done tomorrow.

5. Have a good night's sleep.

Here is an exercise for you to try:

- The next step of forming your winning strategy is to implement a daily ritual into your schedule. Consider your daily schedule and figure out how you can make time for a morning ritual, even if it means waking up earlier. Also determine whether your schedule allows a nighttime ritual and whether you want to have one (although I highly recommend it). If your schedule is sporadic, you can consider creating a customized mid-day ritual that borrows elements from both the morning and nightly ritual to suit your needs. A morning and evening ritual, if done on a regular basis, should greatly increase your productivity, happiness and winning potential!

Eliminate Negative Influences

Humans are easily influenced by outside sources and that in turn can affect our attitudes toward winning, so it is essential to eliminate negative influences from your life as a part of your strategy. You may think of a negative influence as a person or people in your life but you can also be influenced by other factors, such as what you read, what you watch on television and what you see online. Even if you don't think something you see, hear or read will have a conscious impact on you, it could very well have a subconscious impact.

Eliminating negative influences from your life is relatively easy. The first thing you must do is maintain a positive attitude. Those who maintain a positive attitude will find it much easier to "tune out" negativity. Usually when you believe in positivity, it is easy to look at things in a much more attractive light. For example, somebody on your social media friends list may post a negative article, expecting people to feed into it. If you are a positive person, odds are you will just ignore the article and won't be bothered by it.

Here are a few things to remember when trying to practice and maintain a positive attitude:

- Be kind and positive toward anyone in your life who is a complainer. It's usually hard to whine and complain in front of a person who is always so <u>happy</u> and upbeat.

- If somebody around you starts to gossip or say bad things about someone else, simply don't feed into it. Change the topic or focus your attention on something more important.

- Don't be afraid to constructively criticize a person who is being negative. He or she may not realize how negative he or she is being. Sometimes it helps to have an outside source fill you in on how you sound because it is hard to realize it yourself.

The second step you should take is to make a plan on how to avoid negative influences from the media. Media outlets love to publish negative stories because they often generate a huge response from their audience. However, you can easily avoid these outlets and stick to the ones that are more unbiased. A good way to start is to do some research and find out which news outlets in your area publish unbiased stories. If you have friends on your social media accounts who often post negative things, you can easily hide them from your feed without unfriending them. Also try to stick to local newspapers, as these tend to post positive stories. Positive local stories will also help you build a positive connection with your community. If you really want to keep your mind free from all the negative stories out there, simply stop watching the news all together and spend your time reading! You will be much more successful over the long term by doing this and filling your brain with the things you like and would like to learn more about.

The third step is to maintain positive relationships. The people you associate with everyday can have a major influence on you, even if you are not consciously aware of it. Therefore, you should make it your goal – as much as possible – to limit your interactions to positive people. Can you think of any friends who are negative influences? Those types of friends are the kind who put down your goals and ideas by saying things like "Oh that's unrealistic" or "I think that's a waste of time." If any of your friends come to mind, you may want to rethink your friendship with them. You don't necessarily have to break off the friendship, but pay attention to how much time you're spending with that person. It may be necessary to limit your time with a negative person, or dilute their negative impact by surrounding them with a group of positive people.

A good way to spot others who are positive is to look at their habits. Positive people often make it a habit to eat right, exercise and otherwise take care of their bodies. Those who are more apt to lie around and not take care of themselves are usually those who tend to be more negative.

Dealing with negative family members can be a bit more challenging because to most people, family is everything. However, there are some things you can do to manage negative people in your family. One simple tactic is to ask the person why they are so negative. They may have a legitimate reason, one you may be able to help them with. They may be unaware that they come across as negative. By practicing a positive attitude and praising it in others, you will be serving as a role model for your negative family members. However, some people will defend their negativity to the death. If this is the case, and you truly want to be successful, you need to find ways to limit their negative impact on your life.

Here is an exercise for you:

- Think about the negative influences in your life. Do you find yourself often reading or watching negative news stories? Do your friends display positive or negative habits? How about your family members? List the negative influences on your life. Then, decide how you can eliminate or minimize the impact of these negative influences in your life. Writing down your plan is one way to reinforce your goal and show yourself that you take it seriously.

Focusing on the Goal

Goal-setting is an important step in creating and executing a winning strategy. Without a goal, you risk muddling along aimlessly and, ultimately, accomplishing little that has value or meaning.

It is important to consciously choose and actively focus on your goal. It is easy to say: "I'm going to focus and be a winner", but without a solid plan that statement can easily fall apart. A winning attitude alone will not, by itself, make you successful. You need a clearly defined goal and a practical plan to reach it, in order to focus your efforts toward success.

There are two types of goals, short-term and long-term. The long-term goal is your ultimate objective. Short-term goals support your ultimate goal. They break down the goal into more manageable, yet measureable, chunks.

You can pursue several short-term goals at one time. For example, if your long-term goal is to win next year's 20k race, you could pursue short-term goals of specific physical training and healthy eating simultaneously. Some short-term goals must be taken in sequential order. For example, you will not be able to run a 10k race before you are in shape to run a 1k. You will not be able to run a 1k until you can run a block, etc.

Goal-setting consists of several steps that all come together to bring you the best results. Here is how you can easily plan out your goals:

1. Determine your long-term goal, the ultimate desired outcome. In this example, your long-term goal is to be a winner.

2. Make sure that your goal is specific. In the example above, you must clearly define what you want to "win." A vague goal is just as bad as no goal at all, but a specific goal gives you a clear idea of exactly what you need to do to reach it. In your case, your desired outcome is really probably something like "I will easily win first place in the upcoming 5k marathon." Saying "I will easily" at the beginning of each goal helps reinforce your willpower and determination.

3. Figure out what short-term goals you need to set in order to reach your long-term goal. For example, if your long-term goal is to win first place in a race, your short-term goals will probably revolve around taking care of your body and training in preparation for the race.

4. Set a due date for your goal. A due date allows you to scale your plan within it and then you can work backward from your due date. In this way you can assign intermediate dates to your short-term goals and easily keep track of your progress.

5. Write your goal down. According to a research study done at Harvard, a written goal is much more likely to result in its achievement than something that is just in your head. A great strategy that many successful people do is to physically write down their number one goal in the morning on a piece of paper and then at night. I highly recommend you try doing this!

6. Visualize yourself achieving your goal. Visualization is a powerful technique. When you visualize your success, use as many senses as possible. For example, you can easily visualize yourself crossing the finish line of a race as the confetti flies and the crowd goes wild with cheers. Imagine your breath easing after you break the tape, your muscles relaxing. Think of the smell of your favorite food, the taste and feel of it in your mouth as you reward yourself afterwards. Imagine the wonderful feeling of accepting the first place award and how the audience will react. Be as detailed as you can.

7. Think about WHY you want to accomplish your long-term goal. Your "why" is your personal motivator. For example, you may want to win first place in the race so you can show off a trophy or so you can qualify for an even bigger race. And yes, you can have more than one motivator. Everybody's main "why" will be something

different, but it must be strong enough to kick you into gear when you don't feel like leaving the comfort of your warm bed in the morning. A good strategy, when you are feeling unmotivated, is to think of things that will motivate you at this period of time right now.

8. Your goals must be easy to remember and realistic. If you want to win first place in the race but you're really out of shape, it would be unrealistic and next to impossible to reach your goal without first pursuing some major sub-goals. In this case you would need to set up a diet and physical training plan to get you into the shape required to be able to run the race and not die before the finish line. If your goal is to win, you must be able to run first.

9. If possible, find a mentor to keep you accountable for your goals. Unless you're skilled at self-discipline, you may find it helpful to have someone else keeping you in check. A good way to find a mentor is to seek out a person who has the same or similar goals. You can spur each other on as you pursue your individual goals. A person who has achieved the same goal you are now pursuing can also serve as a mentor and cheerleader, reminding you that you *can* do this, because they did it, too. This is a very powerful strategy, so if you can find an accountability

partner it should definitely help you in the achievement of your goals.

10.   Reward yourself.   Celebrate when you've achieved your long-term goal.   It takes a great deal of hard work, dedication, determination and willpower to succeed at a worthwhile goal, so affirm the importance of what you've accomplished. Plan a celebration worthy of your achievement!

Planning a celebration can be a powerful motivator in itself. There is nothing wrong with deciding ahead of time what you want to do to honor your achievement. Then, whenever your goal seems out of reach, imagine yourself in the midst of your achievement party or acquiring whatever else you've chosen as a reward for your success.

Chapter 2: Giving Yourself the Competitive Advantage

Chapter 2 is all about the different things that you can do to give yourself the competitive advantage no matter what your goals may be. These tips are divided into general categories to help you organize your winning strategy.

Health

Eat 3 Healthy Meals per Day

Eating 3 healthy meals per day is a very important step in keeping up your physical health. This may be especially challenging in today's fast-paced world. We can find ourselves pressed for time or too tired before or after work to prepare a healthy meal. The easy solution is to gravitate towards fast food, processed food and pre-packaged, ready-to-eat meals loaded with ingredients that are bad for your body. These foods give you low energy and added pounds which only make it harder to motivate yourself to pursue your goals. You need the opposite. The better shape your body is in, the more likely you are to feel inspired, motivated and confident.

The best foods to stick with are those from the food pyramid: whole grains, fruits and vegetables, meat and poultry, fish, nuts and eggs, milk, yogurt and cheese (with fats and sugars used sparingly). The best way to ensure that you eat healthy meals is to prepare them yourself. If you work odd hours during the day, a good idea is to prepare your meals in advance as much as you can. Many people have also found that the Mediterranean diet is specifically good for feeling your best.

I have also found that eating more frequent and smaller meals is great for your overall energy levels. I would highly recommend eating 4-5 smaller meals throughout the day and just see how much better you feel. If you are looking for some healthy and delicious recipes, be sure to check out my books: Vegetarian Cooking, Gluten Free Recipes & Healthy Meals Recipe Book.

Get Enough Sleep

The amount you can get done in a day is a reflection of how well you sleep. The more you can accomplish in a single block of time, the more likely you are to succeed. The fewer hours you sleep, the more sporadic your sleep patterns are likely to be and the more hours you will end up wasting the next day. Therefore, it is important to get enough sleep and practice good sleeping habits every night.

An adult should get about 8 hours of sleep each night. I've found it best to pick a designated time to go to sleep and to wake up each day. This way, your body can get used to the hours and you won't risk sleeping in after getting too little sleep. I also find that getting up early is helpful because you can often find time to exercise, prepare a nice meal and do other activities that help you become a winner during those hours. You are less likely to be interrupted in the morning because not many people are awake at those hours. This is especially useful for those who have a large and active household.

Eat a Healthy Breakfast

Out of the 3 meals you should eat per day, breakfast is by far the most important. Since breakfast is the first meal of the day, you'll want to eat something that will fill you up but that is also healthy. A good way to ensure that you will stay full until lunch time is to combine protein and fiber. For example, a hardboiled egg with yogurt and a piece of fruit would make an ideal breakfast. Breakfast smoothies are also a good idea because they're easy and quick to make and you can take them on the go.

- Tip for cleaning your blender quickly: Hold your blender upside down and rinse it out. Then pour a little bit of soap and water inside, replace the lid and blend until the soap and water mixture reaches the top. Rinse out again for an easy clean.

Avoid Processed Foods

Processed foods are packaged to be easy and convenient, but that convenience comes with a price. These foods are very unhealthy, often loaded with sugars, carbs, fats and sodium. While they are okay to eat once in a while, you should definitely avoid them in your diet. Stick to healthy, homemade dishes that will leave you feeling energetic and motivated. If you eat a lot of premade and frozen foods and don't have a lot of energy, then start eating more fruits and vegetables instead.

- It's a good idea to avoid eating foods that have a mascot on their brand. These types of foods are often highly processed and full of sugar. Looking out for a mascot can help you quickly determine whether a food is healthy or not.

Exercise with Strength Training and Cardio

Another way to feel great physically and to set yourself up for success is to exercise. Exercising can help you feel energetic, motivated and alive. The main two types of exercise are strength training and cardio. Strength training is important for burning fat, staying strong and it can even help you stay focused, which is a very important part of reaching your goals. Cardio training strengthens your heart and lungs and helps protect your body from diseases, allowing you to remain focused on your goals rather than on your heath.

Strength training exercises can include sit ups, leg lifts, weightlifting, resistance band training or yoga. Here is the bodybuilding routine that has been extremely effective for me over the last fifteen years. It is best to fit each of the following four workouts into an 8 day period. At the very least, all four workouts should be done within a 14 day period. Make strength training a habit and never stop doing it. Ideally you want to take 1 day off after each strength training session. This basic routine has worked great for me. Also, feel free to mix up the exercises if you are more experienced, in order to surprise the muscles and stimulate growth.

Leg Day: I will do a short walk around the block to warm up my legs or jump on a mini trampoline to warm up my legs. I will then stretch out my quadriceps, hamstrings, and calf muscles. After properly stretching, I will start off with 25 squats, using just my body weight to work the muscles. I go nearly all the way to the ground and am careful to use good form. I then do leg extensions with very light weights to further warm up my legs.

Note: I have a Bowflex Revolution, which mimics many of the exercise machines in a gym. This adds the resistance work to many of these routines and provides some variety.

After a short rest of a minute or so, I move on to hamstring curls with around fifteen repetitions using light weights. The final exercise is calf raises. I like to stand on a curb or something similar and use only my calf muscles to lift up my body weight. You need more repetitions for your calves, so I perform about 25 lifts.

This completes one full set of all my leg exercises. I then do all these exercises again, only, now that I am warmed up, I push myself harder increasing the repetitions or I will increase the weight so I work the muscles harder while doing fewer repetitions.

I will then do at least one more complete set of all these exercises, since 3 is the minimum amount of sets you want to do. If I feel like pushing myself, I will do a 4th and 5th set as well. These final two sets are where you will see the most results if you are truly serious about building strength and size. If you are aiming for strength and power, then after the first warm up set, you will want to add more weight and do fewer repetitions.

Arm Day: On this day I work out my biceps, triceps, forearms, and grip strength. After stretching out my arms, I will take some lightweight, free weights and do arm curls with them until I feel a nice burn. I will then take an even lighter dumbbell for the next exercise, called triceps kickbacks. Following that, I work the forearms by doing wrist curls with a dumbbell. I then take a grip strength ball and squeeze it in my hands till I get a nice burn. The final arm exercise is the triceps push down. Near the end of the workout I will typically do a few extra sets of arm curls to really get them strong and looking great. As with all strength training routines, the first set is used as a warm-up, then you push yourself on the remaining sets.

Chest/Back Day: I start off by stretching my chest and back. I will then take some dumbbells and simulate a bench press motion. When my chest muscles are feeling a bit tired, I end the set with dumbbell flies. I then move to a back exercise, called upright rows, using a dumbbell with this as well. I then do another chest exercise called cable crossover, using my Bowflex Revolution, following it with another back exercise called seated rows. After this, I do back hyper extensions or planking for my lower back, then some sit-ups, and finish the first complete set with push-ups. Chest and back day is typically one of the tougher workouts, but it yields great results. Go on to do 2-4 more sets to complete the work out.

Shoulder Day: I start off by stretching out my shoulders. This routine is done exclusively with light free weights. I start the set off with Arnold presses, take a rest, then perform rear lateral dumbbell raises, lateral dumbbell raises and frontal dumbbell raises. I will then use heavier dumbbells and do shoulder shrugs to work the trapezius muscles. As usual, I take a short rest between each exercise set. Go on to do 2-4 more sets to complete the work out.

There a few other things to keep in mind when strength training. You can do your abs and lower back every day, along with your calves. You can exercise your neck muscles daily as well, and it is good to do various motions with your neck to relieve stress and increase strength. It is also a good idea to eat a protein shake or another healthy food high in protein fifteen to thirty minutes after you have completed your workout. My favorite protein shake is Muscle Milk.

Planning your cardio routine is less regimented. Good examples of cardio exercise include swimming, biking, jumping rope, jogging, tennis, basketball, hiking, kickboxing, walking or martial arts. I recommend doing cardio for at least 20 minutes, three to four times per week. Anything below that minimum will not be as effective for peak performance results.

- Lifehack: Try listening to an audiobook while you work out. This way you can accomplish two tasks at once. One builds your physical health while the other stimulates you mentally and spiritually. Some people have reported that listening to an audiobook while exercising has encouraged them to exercise longer (because they want to hear more of the book). You can check out my audio books by going to Amazon and simply typing in: "Ace McCloud Audio" to get a complete list.

Take Vitamins and Supplements

Vitamins and supplements serve as resources to help your body work hard. They can help strengthen your bones, heal your injuries and boost your immune system, all of which can help you stay in great physical and mental shape.

I have personally been taking vitamins, minerals and a variety of supplements for the past twenty-five years. While there are both positive and negative studies about vitamins and minerals, I have had an overall positive experience with them. When I look around and see other people about my age (just over 40), the difference is quite striking. I look younger, I am much stronger, I still have lightning quick reflexes, my skin looks healthy, I still have incredible mental capabilities and I possess overall good physical well-being. Although I'm not a doctor, I think one of the best decisions of my life was to invest in myself, which has included a lot of healthy supplements and vitamins over the years. Of course you have to keep up with exercise and strength training as well.

My strategy has been to give my body all the nutrients it needs in order for it to perform at peak capacity. Over time, you find out which vitamins and minerals and supplements work best for you, and you can discontinue taking the items that may not be having the desired effects. My cabinets are filled with vitamins, minerals, and a variety of other healthy supplements. I try not to take too many at one time. I usually take up to four different supplements after each meal, no more. I have also found it beneficial to take days off from supplementation and to drink lots of water on those days. For more professional results, be sure to make a journal of exactly what you are eating and what supplements you are taking so that you can analyze the results.

Laugh a Little

Focusing on being a winner can turn you into a very serious person. While it is important to be serious about your goals, it is also important to take a step back and laugh a little bit. Laughter truly is one of the best natural medicines for stress relief and physical health, as well as mental, emotional and spiritual well-being. When you choose relationships, look for people with a sense of humor. If you are around others who are funny and lighthearted, you are more likely to find yourself relaxed and enjoying a good laugh. Children and puppies are always fun to watch; a trip to a park or playground can often be highly entertaining. You can also stimulate your own laughter through strategic use of various media. You could watch a funny movie or show, read a funny book (possibly a joke book), download a jokes app on your phone or listen to a comedy podcast. Try to find something to laugh about more than once a day.

De-stress with Aromatherapy

Another great way to de-stress is to utilize aromatherapy. Aromatherapy creates a relaxing environment that allows you to refresh and collect yourself. My favorite way to fill a room with pleasant smelling aromas is with an Aromatherapy Essential

<u>Oil Diffuser</u>. I never liked the heat based delivery systems of other products. By contrast, this one releases a fine mist of sweet smelling aromas and turns off automatically when finished. Some great smelling essential oils you can add to a diffuser or to massage oil are:

- <u>Lavender</u>: known for its relaxing qualities, it smells heavenly too.
- <u>Eucalyptus</u> is a strong, earthy, but pleasant scented plant that is known to help fight inflammation and reduce swelling. It is thought to clear the mind as well.
- <u>Marjoram leaves</u>
- <u>Peppermint</u>
- <u>Chamomile</u>
- <u>Cloves</u>
- <u>Cinnamon Bark</u>
- <u>Sage</u>
- <u>Rosemary</u>
- <u>Cardamom</u>
- <u>Verbena Essential Oil</u>, one of my favorites

- Lifehack: You can use aromatherapy oils to make your car and every room of your house smell good. For your car, put a few drops of oil on a clothespin and clip it to the air vents. To make the rooms in your home smell nice, put some drops of oil onto a cotton ball and place it in your vacuum bag.

De-stress with Meditation

Practicing meditation is a great way to relax your mind and recharge it for a fresh push towards your goals. Meditation involves learning how to focus your attention on something by keeping an open mind and a relaxed posture. Meditation helps stimulate relaxation and good health. Many people practice meditation as a way to reduce their levels of stress, anxiety, depression and insomnia, all of which can drain your energy. Having energy is essential to reaching your long-term goal.

A typical meditation session takes about 20 minutes out of your day. First, you should have a special room or place to meditate. The location you choose to meditate in should be quiet, peaceful, and private. Next, sit in a comfortable position with a straight back. You can sit in any position you like, as long as your back is straight. Set a timer for 20 minutes so you will not be preoccupied with keeping track of the time. Next, close your eyes and start focusing on your breaths. Then, start focusing your thoughts on relaxation. If you begin thinking of anything else, slowly bring your mind back to concentration on relaxing. Meditation will help you balance your emotions and clear your mind.

De-stress by Spending Time Outside

Spending time in nature is another great way to de-stress. There's nothing better than taking a nice walk on a trail, surrounded by tall trees, chirping birds and running water. Many people find themselves better able to relax and unwind in a natural environment.

Take Naps

Finally, sometimes you just have to mentally and physically recharge yourself by taking a nap. While it is important to focus hard on your goal and your winning strategy, sometimes you just need to take 20 minutes or so to close your eyes and let your body naturally recharge itself. I've found that if you try to stay up when you're feeling tired you will not accomplish as much over the long run, if you took a few minutes out for a rest instead. If you don't rest when your body needs it you may end up becoming over-tired and you may later on find it harder to fall asleep at night.

Yoga

Yoga is another relaxing activity that can boost your flexibility and overall positive sense of self. Combine yoga into your daily exercise routine to make the most of your physical strength and boost your energy levels. Yoga is great for increasing concentration, along with joint and muscle flexibility. Yoga can be done very inexpensively: some loose clothing, relaxing music, a soft mat, and internet access or a good yoga instruction book is all you need to get going. The library is a great resource for free books and DVDs on yoga. Or you can join a yoga class. This has the added benefit of social interaction, which has been shown to be important in the prevention of degenerative conditions such as Alzheimer's. Here is a great YouTube link if you are looking for a beginner's lesson on yoga: YouTube Beginners Yoga by Yoga Shala.

Juicing and Smoothies

Juicing and smoothies are a great way to boost your health and increase your immune system. You want to be as strong and healthy as possible so you can focus on achieving your goals and hopefully not worry about fighting illnesses. Using different combinations of ingredients when juicing will help boost your digestive system. Making your own juices will also prevent you from ingesting unhealthy fruit syrups and other processed additives often found in premade products. Homemade smoothies are a quick and healthy meal if you are in a hurry.

One of the best things I have ever done to improve my overall health was to regularly include juicing and smoothies in my diet. I have been using a Juiceman Juicer the past three years and absolutely love it. I just recently added a Nutribullet blender to my routine and am very pleased with that as well.

Incorporating both juicing and smoothies into your diet is a great way to fight the aging process and to give your body quick access to tons of easily digestible vitamins, minerals and nutrients! There are hundreds of recipes out there, with a million ways of combining every sort of vegetable, fruit, and healthy ingredient for a nearly unlimited amount of ways to make healthy smoothies and juices.

I would recommend just taking your favorite healthy foods and juicing them or making a nice smoothie. It really does not need to be an exact science, and honestly, just about every juice drink and smoothie I make with fruits and vegetables tastes pretty good to me.

Here is what I do on a typical day when eating for maximum anti-aging and peak performance. In the morning I make a smoothie of only fruits and vegetables. I do this because fruits and vegetables will digest much quicker if you do not include other proteins with them. My favorite ingredients to use are Spinach, pineapple, green peppers, apples, oranges, bananas, grapes, strawberries, celery, kale, and carrots. Two to three hours later, after I have had my morning walk, I will eat a small meal of almonds, sunflower seeds, and peanuts. I eat primarily almonds, however, as they tend to be the healthiest and give the most energy.

Three or four hours later I will have a regular dinner, and then at night, an hour or two after dinner, I will make a nice juice drink with a huge variety of fruits and vegetables from the list above. I cut up all the fruits and vegetables, run them through the juicer, and get about a quart of juice. I then spend the next thirty minutes or so drinking the results, as it is best consumed immediately after juicing for maximum nutritional benefit. I like to juice after dinner, because if you juice on an empty stomach, it can sometimes cause significant stomach pain. You can also juice smaller amounts of fruits and vegetables if you want to be more economical. At night, around an hour or so before bed time, I will have another light snack or smoothie.

Smoothies are great for giving your body easily digestible foods; they are also incredible for keeping you regular. The same goes for juicing. I have found that smoothies are much less expensive and time consuming, while juicing takes a significantly greater amount of time and money, but really gives you that added boost of energy you may be looking for.

Forgive Those Who Have Wronged You

At some point in your life, another person may have done something to wrong you; this probably has left you with some really negative emotions. I know many people who hold grudges against those who have wronged them for years and years. Those people often focus and dwell on the negative emotions instead of focusing on moving forward. If you are holding any grudges or negative feelings toward anyone in your life, it may be difficult for you to focus on yourself. As part of your winning strategy you should make it a point to forgive any offense you may have toward anyone. Actively choose to let go of the negative and sour emotions you hold toward them. This can make it much easier to move ahead in your life. Holding a grudge can foster feelings of anger and resentment, which can be huge motivation killers.

Forgiveness is not an easy task, especially if a person has deeply hurt your feelings or damaged your life. However, there are some great and therapeutic ways to heal. Sometimes it is as simple as telling your offender how you feel. I can recount many times when I approached somebody who hurt me, just told them how I felt and afterwards we both felt much better. If you're not good at directly approaching people you can also write a letter. Writing a letter gives you time to really organize your thoughts and get your point across without adding any more conflict. Oftentimes, it is even better not to send the letter off. Just writing everything down in letter form can be very therapeutic.

Sometimes forgiveness is as easy as just "letting go." If a person has done something to hurt you but it wasn't a really big deal you can just forgive him or her from within and move on.

Sometimes the person you need to forgive is yourself. We all do things that we aren't proud of; we all make mistakes. Sometimes we are unaware that we have developed hatred and other negative feelings toward ourselves. Forgiving yourself is usually a process that takes time. Here are a few things to remind yourself as you are working through your own forgiveness: nobody is perfect; everybody makes mistakes; pay attention to the circumstances around your issue. Sometimes a little bit of counseling can be extremely helpful. An outside perspective can help you better understand and accept yourself. Also, it's good to know that for the most part, people don't control what thoughts pop into their heads. It's how you deal with those thoughts will help determine if you are playing like a champion or letting those negative thoughts get the best of you. Try focusing your attention on other things that help motivate you.

Forgiveness can take as little as a few minutes or as long as a few months but it is very important to work toward a place where you can forgive and let go. Only then will you be truly free to move toward your goals.

Foster a Healthy Home Life

Home is where you start and end your day, so making sure that you have a heathy and stable home life is important, too. Many view home as the place where they can go to relax and de-stress, so a stressful home environment can really hold you back. I've found that a nice, clean, organized home that smells good all the time is my perfect idea of a home. Each person will have their own preference.

Another important factor to consider is dealing with the people you live with. Sometimes living with one or more people can be difficult, especially if those people are annoying. If you live with a difficult person, there are a few things you can do to reduce the stress:

1. Avoid talking about controversial issues, whether it be the news, politics or even something personal. If the other person brings up a topic that you know is going to lead to conflict, simply change subjects or tell that person you can't talk with them at the moment.

2. Change the way you respond to this person. If he or she starts to nag or get nosy, simply assert that you don't appreciate his or her behavior. Sometimes simply asking that person to change his or her behavior works wonders.

3. Avoid looking for flaws in your roommate. Sometimes focusing on what's bad about a person can conjure up negative feelings, which show up in conversation. Instead, think of some good things about him or her and try to try to find the benefits in living together.

4. Give each other some space. Being on top of people 24/7 can get really frustrating. Everybody needs their own breathing room for a while. Giving each other space is also a great reason to go out, take a nice walk, do some exercising or engage in any other activity that can push you toward your goal.

Habits

Be Consistent in your Endeavors

To have a successful winning strategy, you absolutely must stay consistent in your endeavors. This takes an insane amount of willpower and determination, but the outcome is often worth the hard work. If you are not consistent, then your ability to perform can fluctuate and you're more than likely to drift off course from your goals. For example, if your goal is to win that marathon but you only exercise and train here and there, odds are you will not come in first place. However, if you have a strict schedule for training, you are more likely to have a chance at winning the race. If you're going up for a promotion at work but you only show your abilities here and there and mess up in between, odds are that your superiors will notice you're not consistent and you will be less likely to award you the position. Consistency goes a long way. It's noticeable, it's inspiring, and it works.

- How can you be consistent in your everyday actions to achieve your long-term goal? List three things that you currently do in conjunction with your goal that you can change to be more consistent.

Write Down Your Goals

Writing down your goals makes you 42% more likely to achieve them – that's a big percentage! Writing your goals down makes them clear and specific. It makes them concrete; you have something tangible to look at, a reminder of what you have decided is important. Having your goals written down where you can see them motivates you to actively pursue them.

When you write something down, it's more likely to stick in your mind. Writing down your goals can help keep you on track. You may commit to one long-term goal but find yourself faced with another good opportunity. When you've written down your goals, you're more likely to focus on achieving that one thing before you go after something else.

Finally, writing your goal down is part of the visualization process – when you write a goal down and record it, you can literally see your progress. I personally like to keep journals of the most important areas of my life. In these journals, I write my goals down as well as talk about other details pertaining to my goals. I like to flip back every so often and read through the journal to see just how far I've come!

Eliminate Temptations

Eliminating any temptations that may prevent you from being #1 is another key step in creating a winning strategy. Life is full of temptations; it is easy to blow off something important in the long run for something that is instantly gratifying. However, you usually get the better result when you focus on the things that are geared toward the long run. For example you may want to eat a bowl of chocolate ice cream while you're preparing for the marathon but you know that it will not build your health.

Here's an exercise for you to try:
- Think about your goal and any temptations that might be in your life. How can you eliminate them? Go ahead and make a plan to eliminate all distractions and temptations that will hinder you from achieving your goal and then implement it.

Work toward Your Goal with a Friend

Accountability in goal setting is almost guaranteed to help you reach your desired outcome. While some people are naturally self-accountable, I've found it always better to have a friend or mentor to hold you accountable. It is much harder to let down a friend than yourself, so this strategy often works well. You don't have to meet with your accountability partner – you can always call on the phone, text or keep in contact over social media.

Here's an exercise for you to try:

- Can you think of anyone in your life who would make a good accountability partner? Brainstorm names, then chose the top three people and make it a point to ask them to be your accountability partners. If you can find somebody who is working toward the same or similar goal as you, that makes it even better! Be sure to tell each other your goals and then hold each other accountable when the time comes.

Eliminate Motivation Killers

Motivation is what will carry you from start to finish, so it's a really important element in your winning strategy! To make the most of motivation you should avoid things that kill it. Motivation killers are draining and can leave you feeling discouraged. Here are some of the most common motivation killers:

1. **Ungratefulness** – When you're ungrateful for the things you have in life, it is easy to lose sight of the things that really matter to you. Always take a few minutes every day to remind yourself of what you're grateful for. This exercise can actually add to your motivation as well as your happiness levels.

2. **Jealousy** – Jealously is a big time-waster in addition to a motivation killer. Instead of spending time obsessing over what you *don't* have, spend your time working toward what you want so that you *do* have it. Being jealous of a person doesn't get you closer to what you want. Only your hard work will get you there.

3. **Impatience** – Impatience is another time-waster/motivation killer. Along with impatience comes rushing and when you rush, you're more likely to make mistakes or forget important details. While it is good to want to race after your goals, you should always work at a steady pace. This is a marathon race you are in, not a quick sprint, so pace yourself. I find it helpful to take regular breaks. Take as many breaks as you need in order to stay focused – breaks really do make a difference.

4. **Overwhelming Feelings** – When you start to feel like things are spinning out of control, you are more likely to just buckle under the pressure and give up. However, giving up is never an option if you want to be a winner! Whenever you're feeling overwhelmed, take a step back, take a deep breath and reevaluate your life. Determine what things take priority and what things you can put on the back burner or discard entirely. Organizing your life, physically or

mentally, is a great way to reduce the pressure. Sometimes something as simple as cleaning your desk can help you feel relaxed and in control.

5. **Unhealthiness** – You already know by now that being physically unhealthy can really hold you back. Being healthy is not only important to your motivation, but is the basic building block for the greatest achievers throughout human history!

6. **Fear** – Fear is probably one of the biggest, if not *the* biggest motivation killers of them all. I will touch more upon the topic of fear a little later in this book, but as President F. D. Roosevelt once famously said, "The only thing to fear is fear itself." If you don't know how to manage fear it can hold you back from some of the best opportunities and great moments in your life. Unfortunately, fear is a very strong emotion that can easily get the best of people sometimes. On the bright side, there are some great ways to conquer your fears once and for all, which you will discover in just a few pages!

Start Out with a Small Strategy

Start out small when you're putting together a winning strategy. It is impossible to change overnight, so it is unrealistic to expect an instant transformation. Trying to change everything at once can be overwhelming. As you just discovered, feeling overwhelmed can kill your goals. So, start out small and work your way up. For example, if you're trying to win a marathon but you're totally unprepared, start out by changing your diet. Once you start to feel healthier, start implementing an exercise plan. After you've got that down, start making a plan that you think will get you to the finish line first. Little by little you will master the skills you will need to run a good marathon.

Since it is a very good idea to start small, it is also important to learn how to manage your time wisely. If you are preparing yourself for a marathon, it could take at least 6 months to a year to get yourself in good enough shape. Time management skills are important for creating a winning strategy as well as being successful in other areas of life.

A good way to begin focusing on time management is to become aware of how much time you're spending on each task that leads to your goal. Time yourself on each task and analyze your times every week to see where you're doing well and where you need improvement.

You should also set deadlines for yourself. Having a deadline is motivational and can help you stay on track. Be sure to actually follow up on your times – doing so will ensure that you stay productive.

Finally, if you need help with something, don't be afraid to ask. If you're really confused or unsure about how to perform a task, fretting about it is just another time-waster. Be honest. Accept that you're unsure and ask for help. This can save time by shortening your learning curve. It will also prevent you from wasting time trying to figure things out by yourself.

- **Lifehack**: Turn off all notification alerts on your smart phone (email, social media, text messages, etc). Not only can they be distracting, but knowing you have an unread message will tempt you to read it instead of doing something more productive with your time. Turn your notifications back on when you're finished with all your important tasks.

Keep To-Do Lists

To-Do lists are great tools for helping you stay focused. I love keeping to-do lists, especially when I have a very complex task ahead of me. This way I know that I will never forget to do something important. There are many ways that you can keep a to-do list, depending on what your task is or where you are doing it. You can simply use a pen and paper and carry it around with you for tasks that you are completing within a few hours. If you have access to your computer you can keep your to-do list in a word processor or on <u>Microsoft OneNote</u>. My favorite to-do list computer-based tool is the program, OneNote. This application enables you to easily make to-do lists that correlate with any notes you have; it has a feature that allows you to manually check off each task as you complete it.

Finish Any Tasks/Goals You Start

Winners finish everything they start! Although it can be tempting to switch from one task/goal to another, doing so can actually reduce the chances that you will finish. Remember to focus on one thing at a time. Don't move on to anything new unless you've completed your last task 100%, although occasional breaks are ok. This ensures that you're getting the most out of your tasks and that you will not leave anything behind.

Set Yourself Up For Success

Winners also set themselves up for success! You set yourself up for success by clearing the decks of anything that would slow down your progress and setting the stage for your next efforts. How you will need to set yourself up depends on your individual goal(s), but this strategy will help you stay ahead of the game. For example, if I were preparing to run a marathon, I would come up with a plan to set myself up for the night before my training day that looked something like this:

- Lay out my clothes, shoes, toothbrush/toothpaste, and anything else I will need to get ready in the morning.

- Prepare my breakfast ahead of time if possible and leave it on the counter or in the fridge for quick and easy access. Have anything else needed for the event all ready to go.

- Do anything small that I can in the time left over before bed (for example I could review my goals journal, read a chapter of a book, visualize, etc). This relieves me of having to do it in the morning.

- Go to bed and wake up at a preset, designated time to ensure I am at my most energetic the next day.

- This leaves time for me to train in the morning without being held down by getting ready for the day.

Break Bad Habits that Will Keep You from Winning

After you've repeated an action for about 21 days or so, your brain is programmed to make that action a habit. Some actions you repeat are beneficial, while other actions may not add anything to your life; they may even hold you back from being successful. If you want to be a winner, you should break any bad habits that are holding you back. If I was training to win the marathon but I was a smoker, I'd definitely want to break that bad habit. I'd need my lungs to be strong and fully functioning if I intend to run.

Breaking a bad habit can be difficult, especially if you've been repeating this habit for years. Luckily, there are some steps you can take to make the process a little easier:

Always stay consistent when trying to unlearn a bad habit. To form a habit, you consistently repeated the same action for at least 21 days; to break a habit will take much longer, so you have to be strict with yourself.

It's also a good idea to write about it – you remember how effective it is to right down your goals, right? If you're keeping a goals journal you can write it down in there.

Next, visualize yourself without that bad habit. Think of how great and amazing you'll feel once you've stopped doing something detrimental. If your habit involves something tangible, like food, cigarettes, beer, etc., you can help yourself break that habit by eliminating your temptations. Don't keep anything destructive around you or in your house. Removing them and avoiding places that have them are two great ways to set yourself up for success.

Another great way to help break a bad habit is to find a substitute activity. If you find yourself craving a cigarette, chew some gum. If you find yourself craving junk food, go for a quick jog. Stay consistent with these substitute activities to make it even easier to change. Finally, you could develop a trigger to help you break a bad habit. A trigger is a signal that tells your brain to do something at a certain time. For example, if you want to stop smoking, you can snap your fingers anytime you feel the urge to smoke. If you continue to repeat this action, your brain will eventually associate finger snapping with not smoking.

Lifehack: Do small tasks with your weak hand. (For example, if you're right-handed, use your left hand). Do this for things such as brushing your teeth, eating, using the remote control, etc. Doing this can help re-wire your brain to better learn positive habits.

Self-Discipline

Learn to Persuade Yourself

Sometimes you might find it hard to believe things about yourself that are true. Many people often believe statements about themselves such as, "I can't be a winner," or "I could never achieve my goals", but those thoughts are untrue; they will only hold you back from some of the best opportunities of your life. By learning how to persuade yourself, you can feel more confident and inspired to achieve your goals. You will also learn how to eliminate thoughts that are not true. Persuasion is a great communication skill to have in general and here's how you can exercise it:

1. Focus on what's in it for you. Zoom in on how much your life will improve once you've achieved or acquired whatever it is that you want. If you think you could never win a race, focus on the great feelings of success and accomplishment that you can feel when you do win. Think about how much people will admire you and respect your hard work. Visualize this success.

2. Think about how it helped others in the past. Do some research to find role models. You may stumble across another marathon winner who also thought he or she could not win. By learning their story you may feel more inspired to go after what you want.

3. Research the facts or figures surrounding what you want and make a plan. Those who actually do research and make a plan are much more likely to achieve their goals!

Learn to Influence Yourself

Influence is just as important as persuasion. Odds are that you have been influenced at some point in time by a friend, or by something you saw in the media or have read. Knowing how to influence yourself is even more important because you are the only person who knows you best. Knowing how to influence yourself and others is also a valuable communication skill; you will need to use this throughout your life, both on yourself and to persuade others.

Influence yourself by empowerment. For example, if you resist acting out a bad habit, reward yourself with something nice like a massage or a new piece of jewelry, something that appeals to you. By doing this, you are influencing yourself to stay on track. You can also use logic to influence yourself. When something is logical and makes sense to you it is usually right. If you discover that your chances of winning a marathon are better when you don't eat junk food, you will likely choose to avoid unhealthy foods.

Fuel Your Willpower

Willpower is your third ingredient for personal success, along with persuasion and influence. Willpower is the ability to resist short-term temptations that will have a negative effect on your long-term goal. Willpower is everything in a winning strategy! Willpower is often what sets the winner apart from the losers; winners are more likely to refuse to give up, even amid failures, until they win. Losers often give up immediately after the first or second try. To be a winner you must know how to fuel your willpower.

One of the most important and effective ways to fuel your willpower is – no surprise –a healthy diet. If your blood glucose level is low you are less likely to exert your willpower. If it is too high, you are more likely to have to deal with serious health issues that can also limit your ability to exert your willpower. The best way to balance your blood glucose level is to avoid sugary foods, always opt for whole-grain bread/cereal, and eat plenty of fruits and vegetables.

A good mood also enables you to exert more willpower. This should be easier, since part of your winning strategy is to have a positive mindset. Your positive mindset should help put you in a good mood most of the time of if you are doing things right. It also helps to be happy with yourself. No matter who you are, where you live or what you do, it is 100% possible to be happy. Unhappy people tend to have a negative mindset and rain on other peoples' parades; this makes them increasingly less likeable. If you are not happy, you may want to take a step back and reprioritize some things in your life. Finally, keep working on your laugh; a good chortle can put you and those around you in a good mood all by itself!

- **Lifehack**: Eating foods such as oatmeal, salmon, cereal, milk, bananas and dark chocolate are known to help boost your mood.

- Make a list of things that sometimes make you unhappy. Be completely honest with yourself, otherwise this exercise may not be as effective. Once you've completed the list, think about how you can reprioritize your life to make some positive changes. At the same time, think of some items/hobbies/habits you can add to the list to help you stay in a positive mindset.

Raise Your Standards

When working toward your long-term goal, be sure to raise your standards. Part of working towards a goal is to make it a challenge so that you can push yourself further than before. If you don't challenge yourself or push yourself to go just a little bit further than last time, then you're not really making much of a difference in your life. I find it easiest to have a mentor who can help you raise your standards. Some people struggle with challenging themselves, but I've found that if you develop a mentorship with somebody you really admire and he or she challenges you, it is much harder to let that person down than yourself. You can also join a mastermind group in the area you want to excel at, where you all can keep each other accountable and motivated.

Embrace Change and Adjust Your Strategy Accordingly

Change can be a great thing, but it can also hold many people back from being winners. Some people oppose change because it challenges the status quo – their comfort zone. However, change can sometimes be a really great thing. Take my friend, for example:

My friend grew up across the street from a little family-owned convenience store. It was a unique little shop with a lot of novelty items from the 90's still on the shelf. It was an unspoken rule around our neighborhood that you never bought milk or any other perishable items from that store because they were often expired. Yet, for my friend, it was a sliver of her childhood that never changed. When she found out that the family who owned it had sold the store to new owners, she was really sad because it would mean a huge change. She was reluctant to return to that store, but when she did she found herself pleasantly surprised. The new owners had totally redone the shop, utilizing the space well so they could sell all sorts of new and fresh items. On top of that, the new owners turned out to be really nice people. Now she looks forward to going in there because of all the new great things she can buy. The moral of the story is that even though my friend was saddened by the change of owners, she gave the new owners a chance and found out that it was a change for the better.

Change is really important in today's world. You've probably heard of trending topics – topics that stay popular for a short time and then fall off, replaced by something new. If businesses were to only take advantage of one trending topic and not follow the next one, that business would probably fail sooner rather than later. If a runner wanted to be a great marathon winner but did not change his or her diet, he or she would not be able to do it. Yes, change can be scary, but it can also be really important.

Make it part of your winning strategy to accept and embrace change. A good way to do this is to mentally prepare for it first. Winners are constantly growing and improving, so tell yourself that you know you will face change. The good news is that winners often face positive change rather than negative change, so this can make it much easier. If you're just starting out on your goals and you are afraid you won't like the changes you may face, try to use some visualization techniques to envision how you will feel after the changes occur.

Pushing Yourself to Make Sacrifices

With great reward comes great sacrifice. Living the easy life (i.e. avoiding hard and boring work, sleeping in, not pushing ahead) is what some people want and it's very easy to do. While there is nothing wrong with living the "easy life," it is also a very good way to live a wasteful life and die much younger.

To reach your dreams and truly get rewarded, you will have to make sacrifices. That might mean you choose to get up a little earlier than usual or you choose to give up your TV time. Even though it may feel like you're giving up something you love, the reward is often ten times greater. Just getting up a little earlier can lead to a raise which may eventually lead to you buying that house you really want.

Many have found it helpful to use visualization when making sacrifices. Visualize yourself giving up the activity. Compare it with your goal and see which one looks better. Here is a good way to really put your goals and sacrifices into perspective:

1. Grab a blank sheet of paper or your goals journal.

2. Write this statement: "When I sacrifice (x), my goal (y) will become my reality."

3. Next write the due date for this goal.

4. Finally write out some positive affirmations such as "I will easily make and embrace these changes."

Writing this exercise down helps you make an even stronger commitment to making sacrifices. Think of this as your written contract.

Confidence

Think About Your Strengths

Focusing on your strengths can give you a sense of high self-confidence, which is another key to being a winner. Even strengths that you think are unrelated to your goal can help you. For example, you may be afraid that you will not do well in the marathon, but you're actually a really good planner. So logically speaking, your strong planning skills can serve as a reinforcement of your skill of reaching achievements.

- Think about your long-term goal and your best strengths. How can you apply one or more of your best strengths to your long-term or short-term goals? Be sure to think of the most important aspect that you can focus on that will give you the most positive results.

Think About Your Positive Experiences

If you find yourself needing a little motivational push, you can always think about some of your past positive experiences. All too often people focus more on their negative experiences and that often shifts their current focus negatively. Positive experiences are much more inspirational. For example, you should not think about the time you made a mistake at work, the time you got into an argument with a friend or the time you gave up on something important as part of your winning strategy. Instead, think about the time you helped somebody in need, excelled at something important at work, or finally completed a complicated task. Reflecting on those thoughts can help you feel much better about yourself. If you find yourself drifting toward negative experiences, think about what you learned from them and how you can use those experiences to improve for next time.

- Take out a piece of paper or grab your goals journal and brainstorm a list of some of the most positive experiences of your life. The list can be as long or as short as you'd like. Think really hard and only write about powerful experiences that really left a good effect on you. Refer to this list or chapter in your journal any time you need some feel-good motivation.

Block Out Negative Thoughts

If you find yourself thinking about negativity too much, your strategy can be doomed. To prevent this from happening, you can literally block out negative thoughts. It can be as simple as saying "stop" out loud when you start to think of them. By saying "stop" or another trigger word out loud, your brain will likely become conditioned to associate stopping the action with your negative thoughts. You can also have a happy memory or thought that you can automatically go to when you feel a negative thought coming in.

Have Good Posture

A great way to feel like a winner is to practice good posture. Slouching or slumping over can make you feel less confident and more discouraged. When you stand tall it can make you feel more proud and those feelings can be very motivating. Good posture also promotes deep breathing, which in turn can increase alertness and stimulate feel good endorphins.

Dress Sharply

Another way to be a confident winner is to dress sharply. Dressing well can strongly influence the way you perceive yourself and it can empower you. You don't have to go out every day looking like you're ready to attend an important business meeting, but you should avoid wearing clothes that are dirty, ripped, wrinkled, smelly, etc. Aim to make yourself look presentable. If possible, buy yourself a new outfit or two. I find that whenever I buy a new outfit I tend to feel much more empowered and motivated to do something great.

- **Lifehack**: Sometimes you may end up with an ink stain on one of your nicest shirts! Instead of throwing that shirt away, apply some toothpaste to the stain, let it dry and then wash the shirt. The stain should come right out. Men can also use a hair straightener to iron their shirt collars if they come out wrinkled.

Stay Up To Date on Education

Winners are often on top of their education. Since the world is always changing and evolving, so is education. What you learned in high school may not be relevant today. Fortunately, modern technology allows you to stay educated without even having to set foot in a classroom. There are many free resources available online where you can learn a language, read about a topic that interests you, do research and much more. Many business leaders stay on top of their education; this allows them to catch on to new trends early. I think it is a great idea to imitate these leaders because in a world where trends frequently change, staying on top of the game is both important and challenging. Be sure to keep reading on subjects that interest you and you can also get some great learning courses at www.udemy.com.

Prepare To Stay Strong under Pressure

Pressure and stress often follow winning. Make it part of your strategy to mentally prepare for these. Pressure and stress are often unavoidable, so it is better to know how to deal with them rather than try to avoid them at all costs. Simply knowing that you will eventually run into these two realities is a good starting point for mental preparation. If you fold too easily under pressure, odds are you will not be successful in your endeavors. If you know what specific types of pressure and stress you may incur, it can be even easier to mentally prepare yourself. A good way to find out about specifics is to ask somebody who has already been in your shoes.

Develop a Support System

Developing a support system can be very helpful in creating your winning strategy. When you have the support of people around you, it is much easier to win and accomplish your goals. When you don't have the support of the people around you, it can be very discouraging and tiring. Sometimes those who do not support you will go so far as to constantly talk you down; that can be really discouraging for those who are struggling to maintain their willpower. Having a strong support system is important for maintaining high self-confidence. Think back to Chapter 1 where I discussed how important it is to keep only positive influences in your life.

One thing I didn't touch upon in Chapter 1 was that you should also look for people who will provide you with tough love. A mentor or a coach is often a good source of tough love. This type of person will often keep pushing you to perform at your best, even when you think you can't get any better. A mentor or coach is less likely to let you "slide" when he or she knows that you can do better. Best of all, your mentor or coach was likely once in your position, so he or she will have the experience and knowledge to help you become the best. Think about it, the majority of all peak performers in the world have a great coach or leader influencing them.

Goal-Setting

The 80/20 Principle

The 80/20 Principle, also known as the Pareto Principle, theorizes that 20% of your actions will account for 80% of your success. The 80/20 Principle is a great way for you to prioritize the tasks that support your winning strategy. As you may have noticed, this book discusses a host of different pointers and tips to help you create a winning strategy; it may seem overwhelming at first. This is where the 80/20 Principle comes into play. You can use this principle to determine what the most important 20% of your actions are that will yield the most desirable results, then you can focus on and prioritize these items. This rule is very powerful! It will help you determine what to focus on the most and what to push off to the side for now.

Whether you're applying the 80/20 Principle to your to-do list or your list of goals, you should first determine the 20% of those items that can get you the most results. Be sure to use your judgement on which tasks are more time efficient. This leaves you extra time to get everything you want done. To make this principle easy to understand, think of it this way: Focus on what matters the most. Once you master the

80/20 Principle, you will likely find that your time management skills will have improved. You may be shocked at the incredible results people who use this principle on a regular basis achieve!

Achieve Your Goal with a Plan

Your winning strategy needs to be planned out; otherwise it will probably not work. Creating a solid strategic plan will help you move from where you currently are to where you want to be. Think of it like riding a bike as opposed to driving a car. Riding a bike is like going to point B without a plan – you'll get there, but if you're driving a car (which represents having a plan), you can get there much faster.

Having a solid plan can save you both time and money. The great thing about having your own plan is that you can change it whenever you want. If you find that something is not working or holding you back, you can reevaluate the plan to see where you need to make changes.

Visualization Techniques

I mentioned earlier how important visualization is in terms of goal-setting. Mental imagery is a powerful tool. When you imagine achieving your goal, your brain physiologically creates a pattern that tricks your brain into thinking you've physically achieved it. Visualizing something in your mind helps your body to physically imitate those patterns. Many people who participate in sports use visualization to reach their goals. Visualization also promotes self-confidence and good mood, both of which are key to executing a winning strategy.

Here is a good, basic way to use visualization in achieving your goals:

- Go somewhere you can relax and be alone for a while. This may be your bedroom, office or somewhere in nature. Close your eyes and start thinking about what it is that you want to achieve.

- Breathe in and out deeply and let all tension leave your body.

- Start visualizing yourself achieving your goal, utilizing every sense possible. Visualize how you will feel, what you will hear, what you will see and even what you will smell. Be as specific and as real as possible. Be sure to visualize all the things you will be doing leading up to the achievement of the goal as well.

- Repeat this ritual at least twice a day for at least fifteen minutes each time.

- Keep repeating this ritual until you've succeeded in reaching your goal.

You may also find this YouTube video helpful: <u>Visualization Techniques – A Meditation to Achieve Your Dreams</u> by Jonathon Parker.

The Power of Focusing

Focusing alone can be an amazing source of motivation and <u>inspiration</u> toward achieving your goals. Anybody can utilize the power of focusing. Focusing allows you to get the most out of the goals you are pursuing by helping you to create a strategy. Part of this strategy is to never give up, even if you've come to a block in the road. When you're focused on your goals and you are faced with an obstacle, you are more likely to persist until you find another way around it. Focusing allows you to create a new strategy or alter the one that you already have.

Another benefit of focusing is that it can eliminate stress-related health problems. When you focus on the positive aspects of your goal, you are less likely to experience stress related health symptoms such as headaches and dizziness. It also helps you to build self-awareness. Focusing encourages creativity and self-development. You will likely find that you have a better sense of yourself and your purpose in life. Focusing enables you to trust yourself and your feelings, to control your relationships and to make the right decisions.

I've found that using <u>Focus Formula</u> has been very beneficial in helping me focus on my goals. It is fairly inexpensive and works great.

Model Your Competition

Modeling your competition is a great way to keep improving yourself. Many see competition as a negative factor, but it is critical for the drive and motivation needed to achieve big things. A good way to model is to check out your competition. Perhaps you notice your competition is much better at doing something than you. Maybe you're doing something a lot less efficiently than they are; this could be a great opportunity to learn from your competition. Take note of what your competition does differently – maybe he or she eats differently, has a different attitude, practices a different ritual, etc. You might even find it easy to approach and talk to your competition if they're willing.

- Think about your own competition in terms of your goals. Think of anything your competitors do differently from you; could this be negatively affecting your performance? Brainstorm a few alternatives and then draw up a plan to start using those changes. Don't feel like you have to imitate everything the competition does, but learn from any practices that are giving them an edge over you and turn them to your own advantage

Balance Your Strengths and Weaknesses

Everybody has strengths and everybody has weaknesses. A single person is rarely good at *everything*. You may be great at writing but awful at editing. You may have a knack for sales but be terrible at content creation. Maybe your catching skills are amazing but your running skills need work. Part of your winning strategy should be to balance your strengths and weaknesses so that you can get the most out of your efforts.

You can balance your strengths and weaknesses in one of two ways, depending on your skills, the situation and your personal preference. The first option is to outsource your weaker skills. Outsourcing is when you pay somebody else to do a certain type of work for you. For example, a person writing a book may actually write the book himself but then outsource the editing work. You can usually find independent contractors who perform specific skills and services you need and for a good price on www.Fiverr.com, www.Elance.com, and www.Odesk.com. Your second option is to work on strengthening your weaknesses. If you are writing a book and need a good editing job, you can strengthen your editing skills by reading books, taking classes and practicing editing.

Outsourcing is usually a faster and more convenient option for balancing your strengths and weaknesses, but in some cases outsourcing won't work. If you are trying to improve your physical performance for a sports competition or if you're trying to improve your weaknesses for a business promotion, you cannot have somebody else do the work for you.

"Never Give Up" Attitude

Maintain a "Never Give Up" attitude at all times – it is one of the best ways to almost always guarantee success. My favorite way of reminding myself to maintain this attitude is to Google or YouTube the term "Never Give Up." You can find lots of great inspirational messages that should keep you motivated. This is a great way to remind yourself to never give up, even when you think you're in a bad position. Here are some other great ways to maintain a "Never Give Up" attitude:

Live in the Present: When you are planning your goals, the present is the most important time to focus on. While it is important to focus on the ultimate objective in the future to one extent, you must remember your present actions are what will get you to the future. Avoid dwelling on the past at all costs, unless you are using a positive past experience for motivation. You cannot change the past; if you dwell on negative past experiences, you will not be able to effectively work on the present.

Say "How Can I" instead of "I Can't": Have you ever given up easily after determining that you couldn't do something? Saying "I can't" is easy, but it is also a cop out. A better way to approach the situation is to say, "How can I?" Turning the negative affirmation into a positive one can help you to brainstorm <u>creative</u> ways to actually achieve what you want. You can change your potential quitting attitude into a real go-getter attitude.

- Make it a habit to start saying "How can I?" instead of "I can't." Next time you find yourself wanting to give up on something, remember to say "How can I?" and see what kind of a difference it makes.

Hypnosis

Some find that hypnosis is an effective strategy for self-improvement. It is a safe way to boost your performance. There are currently several hundred research studies on the benefits of hypnosis. A great way to perform hypnosis today is to use self-hypnosis, where you can simply listen to a track rather than go to an actual hypnotist. One of the best sites to use is <u>HypnosisDownloads.com</u>. I have used this resource many times and have found it very effective. I listen to an audio nearly every day.

Here are some great audios to consider from Hypnosis Downloads:

Be Less Negative

Beat Fear and Anxiety

Increase Productivity

Seeding Success

Quick Confidence

Complete Stress Management

Power Positivity

Stellar Success

Massage

Getting or giving yourself a massage is a great way to stay on top of your game. A massage is very relaxing and is great for stress-relief. I view a massage as the perfect way to rest and recharge so you're ready to perform at your best the next day. Here are a few ways that a massage can be a beneficial part of your strategy:

Eliminate Headaches, Migraines and Tension: A massage is great for eliminating headaches, migraines and tension, all of which may hold you back from performing your best. Since this pain often starts in your head, you can simply eliminate it by giving yourself a massage. One way is to untie your hair if needed and sit on a chair, preferably in front of a mirror. Keeping your fingers wide open, place your hands on your head. Ensure that your fingers are pointing up. Apply light pressure and move your hands upward. Make sure that your palm and fingers do not release the pressure and stay in contact with your head. Repeat the same process for other parts of the head as well. You can increase or decrease pressure as needed.

Another good method is to place one of your hands on your forehead to stabilize your head as you give a vigorous massage with your other hand. Rub your entire head until you've covered it all. You can then change hands and rub as gently or as forcefully as needed. Another option is to slightly massage your head with your fingers. Move your fingers throughout the head and keep rubbing continuously. Finally, you can gather up strands of your hair in your hands and pull them gently. Keep doing this for different parts of your head, and you should feel a nice tension relief.

- **Lifehack**: If you cannot relieve a migraine with a massage, soak both of your hands in ice water while repeatedly opening and closing your fists.

Reduce Bodily Stiffness: Another great benefit of massage is that it eliminates bodily stiffness. Flexibility feels good and it can often make you feel empowered to go out and achieve your goals. A stiff and sore body can be a real motivation killer. Most stiffness occurs in your back and shoulders, a location where it is hard to give yourself a massage. To eliminate stiffness in those areas, I recommend paying for a real massage or investing in some helpful do-it-yourself tools. I personally use a trigger point roller and a rubber ball to get at my back and shoulders.

For arms and hands, you can do this exercise: Take a squeezable, rubber ball and hold it tight in your hand. Squeeze the ball and then release it. Continue doing this until you feel tired. This will improve your grip, make your hands strong and it will also increase the blood circulation to your hands and forearms. To relax your forearm, move your finger down from your elbow about 1 inch. Massage this point to relax your forearm. Finally, you can use your thumb to massage the front and backside of your wrist by using an up and down motion. This will improve blood circulation and help keep your muscles active.

For your legs, try this: lie on the floor face down and place a ball or foam roller in the middle of your upper leg. Then, move your leg up and down by exerting pressure on the muscle. This works great for relieving knee pain and upper leg pain. You can also sit on a chair and place a ball underneath your leg. Move your leg up and down to help get rid of any hamstring pain. If you are watching TV or sitting down almost anywhere, you can very easily massage your legs to help relieve pain and tension.

There are some other good basic ways to massage your lower legs. One easy way to massage them is to sit on a chair, grip the back side of your leg and apply pressure. You don't have to massage it but you need to squeeze the muscles with a good amount of strength. This will release pressure, pain and stress. You can also lie down on your back and place a ball under your lower leg. Then, move your leg slightly back and forth while applying pressure to get rid of any pain. Rubbing your calf is also very helpful in getting rid of fatigue and leg discomfort. You can massage your calf area with or without massage oil, depending on the situation. The front of the calf needs to be massaged as well. You can massage it gently with your thumbs. Another nice way to massage your front calf is with the help of a foam roller. Place the roller on a flat surface and put your front calf on it. Move your foot in and out so that the calf moves on it.

For your feet, try this: Massage the bottom of your foot and apply pressure on the sole. Massage your heel with both thumbs in small circles. You can either do this forcefully or you can do it gently. Another good area to pay attention to is the very center on the bottom of the foot. Don't forget the toes; massage each toe individually to get rid of pain and stress. Slightly pull on the toes and then slide your finger between the toes, while moving your toes back and forth with the help of your hand. You can massage your toes all at once with your hand from the bottom as well as from the top.

Alleviate Stress: Finally, a massage is just a good way in general to alleviate stress. Be sure to create a relaxing atmosphere – a nice dark room with some soft music playing in the background. I highly suggest combining massage with aromatherapy to make it as stress-relieving as possible. Light some nice scented candles or any other nice smelling item and be sure to include your favorite scented lotion.

Overcome Fears

Fear is a negative emotion that can often hold you back from moving forward in life and achieving your goals. Fear can affect you both physically and mentally, so it is important to transform yourself into the most fearless person as possible. Everybody has fears and sometimes you cannot 100% erase them, but you *can* learn how manage and deal with them. The better you can manage and deal with your fears the better chance you have at being a winner. Here are some great ways to do this:

Practice Breathing Techniques

Sometimes a simple breathing technique can be really calming in a physical way. Many people use breathing exercises to control their fears. Deep breathing can slow your heart rate and relax your muscles. Check out this basic breathing exercise:

1. Lie flat on your back, raise your knees and put your feet flat on the floor or on the bed.

2. Place one hand, palm down, on the abdomen right under the ribs and breathe as you normally would for one minute.

3. Relax and breathe deeply in, then out, pausing between each breath. Your hand should rise and fall with each breath. If your shoulders are going up and down instead, you are not using the diaphragm and are not breathing to your full potential. The diaphragm is a circle of muscle that is right under the ribs and goes around your body from front to back. When you breathe in through your nose, your filling lungs push your diaphragm down, raising your hand on your belly. When you exhale through the mouth, your diaphragm will contract back to its original position and your hand will sink back down.

4. Try breathing using the diaphragm. It should be easier lying down than sitting up because

when reclining there is pressure against the back that allows the diaphragm to work better. Your hand goes up and the diaphragm goes out when you inhale and the hand goes down and diaphragm goes in when exhaling.

5. Once you get the idea of breathing correctly, you can continue. You should already feel a bit relaxed. Perform six breaths and hold your breath between the inhale and the exhale. Breathe in and out slowly. Avoid breathing too quickly or overdoing it because you can cause hyperventilation, which can make you feel like you are suffocating or like you are very light-headed. Do this exercise at least once a day and gradually increase from six breaths to 12 breaths over time. Another breathing exercise draws air across the tongue and causes a cool sensation that calms the nervous system. Do it while sitting in a chair or by sitting cross legged on the floor.

List and Research Your Fears

One of the most common and biggest fears is fear of the unknown. The less you know about something the more wary you are. I've found it helpful to list and research my fears. I have found that the more I understand something, the less I fear it. I have a friend who once feared bed bugs. One year there was a bed bug epidemic going around her state and she was absolutely petrified of bringing them into her home. She spent hours researching bed bugs and learned about their science, the signs of them and how to prevent them. After doing all the research, she felt much better because she knew how to be proactive and prevent them.

- Take a blank sheet of paper and list your biggest fears. One by one, I want you to take some time and research those fears. You may be surprised at what you find. You may find out that many other people share those fears, which can be extremely comforting. Find out as much as you can. This can also count as facing your fears; by the time you're done researching, who knows? You may not be as fearful.

Try Hypnosis

If your fears are really severe you may want to give hypnosis a try. At Hypnosisdownloads.com they have some really helpful downloads. Check out the Fears and Phobias page where they have different downloads based on different fears. I also recommend the Beat Fear and Anxiety pack.

Be Organized

Keep Your Home Organized

When your home environment is clean and organized you are more likely to have a fully functioning, healthy life. Since you start and end your day in your home, you should take extra pride in keeping it clean and organized. Make sure you wash your clothes, sheets, etc. on a weekly basis and try to pick wall colors that are soothing. Keeping your bathroom and kitchen clean and organized can also save time and help you feel less stressed. Make your home feel like a place where you would love to be.

- **Lifehack**: Clean out your home before you organize it, otherwise you may just end up with a bunch of organized junk. I've found it helpful to ask myself, "Have I used this item in the last 6 months?" If not, I find myself more inclined to throw it away, sell it, or donate it. Once you've actually condensed your belongings, it is much easier to organize. You will likely find it much easier to foster a winning attitude and relax in your newly organized home.

Keep Your Digital Life Organized

With most of your information stored on the computer and across a host of other electronics, it is important to keep your digital life organized as well. A big part of this means keeping all of your projects organized on your computer. A good way is to have a master folder for each type of media that you have. For example you can have one folder for documents, one folder for videos and one folder for spreadsheets. Alternatively you could have a subfolder in each master folder for subprojects. I also recommend backing up your files on an external hard drive, a USB drive or a digital drive such as iCloud or Dropbox.

I recommend digitizing as much as you can - everything from business cards to your notes. There are many programs available that allow you to scan and save images of business cards or important invitations. I personally love Microsoft OneNote. Using OneNote, you can import handwritten notes and pictures of almost everything; you can attach digital notes to anything you import and organize almost anything.

- **Lifehack**: Always take a picture of a business card that somebody gives you. This allows you to store the information in case you lose the card, plus it can help reduce clutter.

Keep Your Schedule Organized

Having a schedule is important for success but it only works if it is organized. Having a schedule can help you learn how to utilize and maximize your time. I have found that the more time you have and the more "ahead" you feel, the easier it is to succeed. I have found that picking one day to organize your schedule is the best strategy. Include every task that you need to accomplish, from work stuff to personal stuff (grocery shopping, exercising, etc). As you sit down and organize your schedule, think about what you were able to achieve during the previous week. Thinking about your past accomplishments due to scheduling can be really motivating!

Keep Your Budget Organized

Finally, it is important to keep your budget organized. Money issues can be very stressful and can stop you from focusing on your goals. The best way to avoid stressing over money is to make sure that you have managed it properly. A great way to do this is to use the 50-30-20 system. Using this system, you can put aside 50% of your income for living expenses, 30% towards your savings or any debt you need to pay off (credit cards, loans, etc) and 20% toward recreational expenses. Personally, knowing that I have my finances under control allows me to focus more on my goals. It's also helpful for ensuring that you get enough sleep at night.

- **Lifehack**: Take a picture of your fridge and cupboards before going grocery shopping so you can remember what you *don't* need to buy. This can help you to avoid overspending or buying duplicates.

Motivation

Overcome Future Obstacles Now

As with any goal, you will usually run into an obstacle or two along the way. For example, if you're trying to stick to a diet and you go to a Christmas party, your obstacle will probably be all of the delicious-looking foods and desserts that people bring. If your goal is to get a promotion at work, an obstacle might be the pressure to get extra work done in less time or to outperform an ambitious colleague. By thinking about potential obstacles in advance, you can strategize solutions to these problems before they occur. It is much better to be prepared than to realize one day after many hours of work that you didn't anticipate a critical detail and it is going to set you behind dramatically. Take your time to be smart, do your research, and the majority of the time you will come out smelling like roses.

Of course, you may run into an obstacle that you couldn't predict. If that happens, just stay positive and work through it. Maybe you are trying to save money but then your car engine fails. Unfortunately, you probably couldn't foresee that, especially if you have a newer car. Don't get discouraged. One good thing about obstacles is that they make you stronger. By trying to predict and plan for some of the more common obstacles associated with your goals, you will be less likely to get discouraged in the event of a roadblock.

Prepare for Failure

This technique is a little similar to the strategy of trying to predict and plan for obstacles, but it has some unique aspects. As you probably know, sometimes you will not win. Sometimes you will not reach your goal or you won't reach it in the time frame that you wanted. If you start working toward a huge goal with high expectations, just to find out that you won't be able to reach it, you will most likely become very disappointed. To stop yourself from becoming permanently discouraged, prepare in advance to handle failure. Prep yourself to look at failure in a positive light. If you try something and you fail, you may realize that you need to do something differently. Don't view it as a complete loss — view it as a lesson learned. Remind yourself that you will not make the same mistakes in your next venture.

While you shouldn't *"not"* reach for the stars, plan to use any failure to your advantage if it does occur. Sometimes more important things pop up or life just gets in the way. As you have already heard many times before, one of the great keys to success is to just never give up. Keep moving forward with dogged determination, despite any setbacks that may occur along the way; eventually you *will* reach your destination.

Eliminate Excuses

Excuses are a big reason many people fall into the groove of becoming unmotivated. When you continually make excuses for why you are not progressing toward your goals, you are not going to get anywhere. A good way to catch an excuse is to stop yourself when you hear yourself saying, "but." Whenever you hear or feel that word coming off your tongue, stop yourself and don't let the rest of the sentence come out.

For example, if you hear yourself saying, "I really want to put this $20 away for the future but I also really want this new shirt..." immediately recognize that you're making an excuse for not sticking to your goal. Another good idea is to use reverse psychology on your excuses. For example, you could say, "I really want to buy that new shirt but if I do that, I won't reach my goal of saving." (In this case it's ok the use the word "but" as a warning.)

Avoid Jealously and Impatience

Jealously is a huge motivation killer because when you get wrapped up in it, you tend to get caught up on how you don't have something instead of spending that time trying to get it yourself. Most likely, you have friends who just *love* to show off in real life or on social media. Sometimes seeing something on social media is the worst because you automatically think that someone else is living the perfect life while you're not. Any time you are feeling jealous, don't let yourself get wrapped up in it; instead, think about what kind of goals you can set to get the things going the way that *you* want and start to work on them. When you are confident that you will be working toward getting something that you really want, your chances of achieving it will be much higher.

Don't confuse being impatient with having a sense of urgency. If you are impatient, you will not likely get very far in life and it will be very difficult to methodically make progress towards your goals. When you're impatient, you tend to forget things and make more mistakes than if you had slowed down and paid more attention. Sometimes impatience can be hard to tackle because it's different for everybody. One technique that generally helps is to take frequent breaks. Breaks can help you slow down and refocus on whatever you're working on. Another good idea is to think about the great results you can end up with when you exert a little bit of patience. Being impatient can give you a very bad reputation if you are rushing through things, being sloppy, cutting corners and delivering subpar results that could easily have been rectified by taking the time necessary to do the task properly in the first place.

Read Motivational Quotes

I've found that reading motivational quotes can be very helpful to stimulate my inspiration. These days you easily have access to motivational quotes. If you have a smart phone, there are plenty of downloadable apps that let you read motivational quotes. If you have a lot of Facebook friends, you'll likely see somebody posting a motivational quote or two on their timeline every day. There are also many websites that will send motivational quotes to your email daily. Alternatively you could buy a book full of motivational quotes and carry it around with you throughout the day.

Strong Desire to Finish Strong

A strong desire to cross the finish line is an important part of your winning strategy. Strong desire is essential to achieving your goals. You probably have this within you; strong desire is mostly a combination of stubborn determination, sheer willpower and other factors. The struggle for most people is to maintain a strong desire over time. Have you ever been in a situation where you were all revved up, ready to go after something you wanted, and then a few weeks later you found yourself less excited? This is normal; the danger is that as the "honeymoon phase" of your pursuit ends, your desire to win can be replaced with an equally strong desire to give up. This is the time, however, to consciously commit to endure until you have reached your goal. You can help yourself by momentarily focusing on your next sub-goal. Often, the completion of a smaller subtask is all you need to stoke the fires for the long haul. I've also found that the best way to maintain a strong desire to finish is to remind myself why my goal matters.

If your goals don't have a special meaning to you, it is likely that you will not achieve them. For example, you may have a goal to start eating healthy... but why? Perhaps you want to win a marathon or you want to live longer so you can enjoy your grandchildren; maybe you're just tired of feeling "blah." Knowing *why* your goals matter to you helps eliminate the temptation to cheat or give up easily. Any time you find yourself wanting to slack off, just remind yourself of the "why."

- On a piece of paper or in your goals journal, write down a few reasons why your goals matter to you. Writing these reasons down can help you remember them better. Writing them down can also inspire you to brainstorm; you may come up with several new "whys," making the meaning of your goals all the more powerful.

You may also find this YouTube video on motivation helpful: Tony Robbins – The Keys to Massive Success by Ron Henley.

Chapter 3: Gaming Strategies

Many people view goal-setting as a game. Whether you're playing an actual game (sports game, board game, video game, etc.) or you're trying to reach any kind of goal, it can be helpful to view it as a game. There are many components of gaming that you can use to create an ultimate winning strategy. This chapter is all about gaming strategies and how you can use them to stay ahead.

Reading Your Opponent

Whether you are playing a card game, a board game or a sports game, it is very important to know how to read your opponent. By analyzing your opponent's moves, facial expressions and other body language you can often get a good idea of what he or she is thinking. You can then use that information in the context of your game to give yourself an advantage. Learning how to read your opponent borrows factors from both science and psychology. It is a hard skill to learn, but if you can master it, you will often find yourself coming out ahead.

When it comes to card games, the first step in reading your opponent is to read the cards. This allows you to identify the best possible hands. Next, you should watch your opponent's actions during the next couple of rounds and use logic to try and figure out why he or she would make those moves. Try and use that information to work backwards, figuring out what cards he or she might have. Ask yourself questions such as, "How many hands is my opponent playing," "What cards were shown down at the end," "What position is my opponent in," "Is my opponent aggressive or passive," and any other questions you think can help you figure out his or her hand.

When it comes to playing a board game such as chess or checkers, you can also attempt to read your opponent's mind. It is important to carefully watch your opponent's every move, as this can often help you gain an insight into what he or she is thinking. Analyze where every piece is on the board (including your own) and try to put yourself in your opponent's shoes. Ask yourself what you would do in that position.

Finally, you may find it helpful to know how to read your opponent in a sports game. This type of reading is often more intense because players are constantly moving around in a sports game. Watch your opponent as early as possible, to determine his or her strengths and weaknesses. Observe whether your opponent sticks to one part of the court/field or ranges all over, whether he or she knows all the moves of the game or just sticks to a few and whether he or she is aggressive or passive.

Preparing For Your Game/ Practice Makes Perfect

To win a game often takes a great deal of preparation and practice. Preparing for your game will depend on what type of game you are playing. For example, soccer players may prepare for a game by eating plenty of carbs beforehand for a good burst of energy. Other types of games, such as chess, may require more practice as a preparation measure. Practice is paramount, no matter what kind of game you are playing. The more you practice, the more likely you are to become a skilled master.

You can either practice with your team or by yourself. Even if you are playing a sport, there are plenty of ways to practice on your own (e.g., doing layups, practicing goal shots, practicing your serve, etc). In your spare time, it can be helpful to think of ways you can prepare for your game, depending on what type of game it is and what are the surrounding circumstances. For example, if you're preparing to play in a big poker game, it may be more beneficial for you to get a good night's sleep and eat specific foods.

Also be sure to mentally prepare yourself. Visualize yourself winning, prepare positive affirmations or do whatever it takes to get into yourself in a positive mindset. Refer back to some of the previous chapters for good ideas on how to mentally prepare yourself for success. You might also find it helpful to mentally prepare yourself for failure as well, just in case. This can prevent you from becoming discouraged in future games.

Rest Up

No matter what kind of game you're playing, be sure to rest up the night before. Getting a good night's sleep is important, not only for winning but for feeling healthy and strong overall. I've found it helpful to listen to relaxing music as I fall asleep to get rid of any tension or anxiety I may have about an upcoming game. Getting enough sleep can help you gain mental strength, which is very important for staying strong and focused.

- **Lifehack:** Some people find it helpful to blink their eyes really fast for a few minutes while trying to fall asleep. The more tired your eyes are, the more likely it is that you will fall asleep faster. Some people have also reported that it is easier to fall asleep while sleeping on the right side of their body rather than the left.

Have a Strategy in Place

Don't go into your game without a strategy. That often leads to failure. Instead, plan out a good strategy a week or so beforehand and practice it until you feel confident enough to go in strong. Your strategy will differ depending on what kind of game you are playing, but having a strategy is definitely better than having no strategy at all. If you are an experienced player, it will probably be easy for you to craft the best strategy possible. If you're a new player, you may find it harder to craft one. In that case, I would recommend talking to other experienced players or watching some good YouTube videos to help you come up with a solid strategy. Once you become more experienced, you can adjust and tweak your strategy as needed.

Stay Hydrated

Staying hydrated is very important for gaming, especially when you're under pressure. Drinking enough water can prevent dry mouth, keep your body cooled down and get help to get rid of any negative toxins from your body. It also promotes good cardiovascular health and promotes the healthy function of your muscles and joints. Even if you don't feel thirsty, drinking water can often help you feel refreshed and able to focus. Never go into a game without having a couple bottles of water on hand.

Model Yourself after Experts

As a former pro gamer, I believe that there is always room for improvement, no matter how long you've been playing. I've found it especially helpful to model myself after experts. See if you can team up with a more experienced player who is willing to help you learn some new things. More than likely, a fellow gamer will be willing to help you out. I've also found it helpful to watch YouTube videos of experts. YouTube usually has a good selection of how-to videos that can help you improve your game.

Play With Those Who Are Better Than You (Learning Experience)

Don't be afraid to play with those who are better than you. View it as a challenge and learn from those players. If you never challenge yourself, chances are that you will never improve your game. A great idea is to play with those who are more experienced and then ask them to critique you, as they can often give you some good insight into what you're doing right or wrong.

Avoid Playing When Stressed Out

If you find yourself really stressed out, then avoid playing. Stress can dull your emotions and limit your ability to make sound decisions; this can be really ugly if you have a tie game or you are playing a game like poker. It can also knock down your physical health by causing headaches, low energy levels, upset stomach or chest pain. There's nothing more dangerous than going into a game when you're already agitated and then something happens to increase that agitation. The best way to avoid feelings of stress before a game is to do something peaceful and relaxing beforehand. I've found that listening to music helps me relax, but you can do anything that works for you. Refer back to the previous chapter for some great ideas on how to relax.

Strengthen Hand-Eye Coordination

Many games require good hand-eye coordination, the ability to coordinate your hand movements with your eyes. Many sports and video games require excellent hand-eye coordination due to constant movement. If you are a person who engages in action games such as sports, it can be helpful to practice some hand-eye coordination exercises.

Exercise #1: Hold a tennis racket with your palm pointing up. Try to bounce a ball on it 25 times without missing or moving your feet. Then point your palm down and repeat.

Exercise #2: Use a bouncy ball, such as a tennis ball, and throw it against a hard surface, such as a brick wall, catching it every time. Alternatively, you can practice catching with a partner.

Exercise #3: Play a video game! Playing video games is a fun way to improve hand-eye coordination, because you need to use your hands to control the main character while paying attention to what's happening on the screen. It is also good for honing your competitive nature.

After you win, it's always a good idea to be a gracious winner and to not gloat too much. While it can be extremely fun to rub it into other people's faces, for your long term success and friendships, it is better to be gracious when you win. The true professionals have learned that being a good winner goes a long way towards building up your reputation as someone people can look up to.

Conclusion

I hope this book was able to give you some ideas as to how you can create some winning strategies for reaching your dreams and goals.

The next step is to execute your game plan.

You are now aware of the steps you should take to create the ultimate winning strategy for your goals. Now is your chance to put everything together. Your winning strategy will always be unique, depending on what your goals are, because everybody is different. Take the top five things you have discovered in this book and start using them. After you have mastered these, choose five more things to work on. Be sure to make a plan and to execute it while being as smart and healthy as possible.

The best way to ensure that you execute your game plan in the best way possible is to hold yourself accountable (or have somebody else hold you accountable). Hold yourself accountable for results and behavior. Remind yourself that you are in control of your life and that you want the best results possible. I've found it helpful to make sure that your plan has a nice flow. If your plan is all over the place, you are more likely to fail. Remember how important organization is? Start with your short-term goals and slowly work your way through them until you've reached your long-term goal. Start with the most basic short-term goal, the most fundamental skill you need to sharpen, then move to the next, building each skill upon the one before it.

Make sure you are truly passionate about your goals. This makes it ten times easier to execute your game plan. Think back to why your goals matter to you and what benefits will come from reaching them. Don't be afraid to create rituals, make yourself accessible to valuable resources and most importantly, be yourself.

Never begin a winning strategy without at least one goal in mind! Review your progress at least once a week, if not more, to ensure that you are staying on track and making the most of your time. Don't be afraid to change your course if something isn't working out. You will likely find yourself faced with a lot of trial and error, especially if this is your first time creating a strategy. Experiment until you find what works best.

Finally, celebrate your achievement. It doesn't have to be a celebration of your final goal – in fact, I recommend celebrating every step of achievement along the way. Celebration and rewarding yourself is a great way to stay motivated, feel good and strive to keep going.

Now it's your turn! Take some action and achieve your goals!

Finally, if you discovered at least one thing that has helped you or that you think would be beneficial to someone else, be sure to take a few seconds to easily post a quick positive review. As an author, your positive feedback is desperately needed. Your highly valuable five star reviews are like a river of golden joy flowing through a sunny forest of mighty trees and beautiful flowers! *To do your good deed in making the world a better place by helping others with your valuable insight, just leave a nice review.*

Thanks and Best of Luck

My Other Books and Audio Books
www.AcesEbooks.com

Peak Performance Books

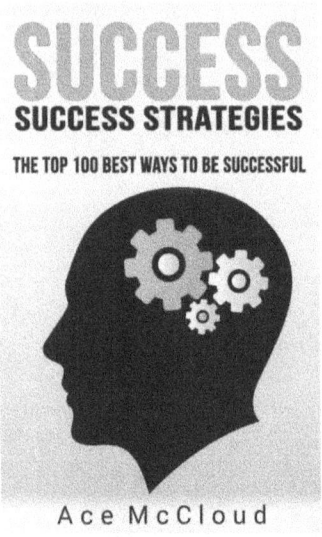

SUCCESS

SUCCESS STRATEGIES

THE TOP 100 BEST WAYS TO BE SUCCESSFUL

Ace McCloud

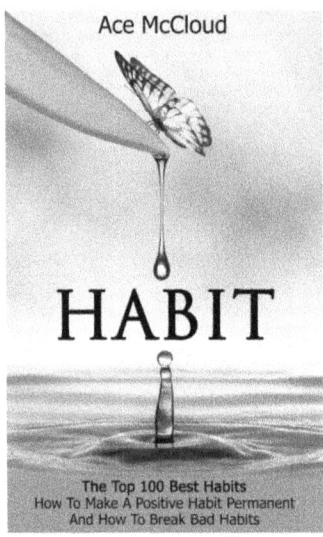

Ace McCloud

HABIT

The Top 100 Best Habits
How To Make A Positive Habit Permanent
And How To Break Bad Habits

MOTIVATION

MASTER THE POWER OF MOTIVATION
TO PROPEL YOURSELF TO SUCCESS

Ace McCloud

ATTITUDE

Discover The True Power Of
A Positive Attitude

Ace McCloud

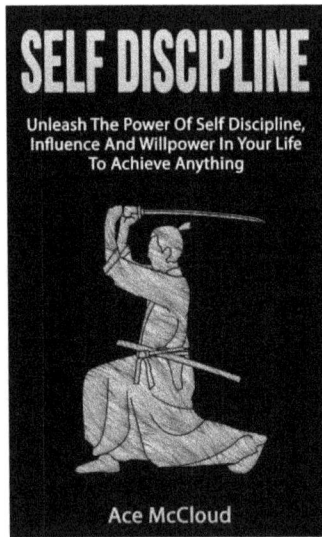

SELF DISCIPLINE

Unleash The Power Of Self Discipline,
Influence And Willpower In Your Life
To Achieve Anything

Ace McCloud

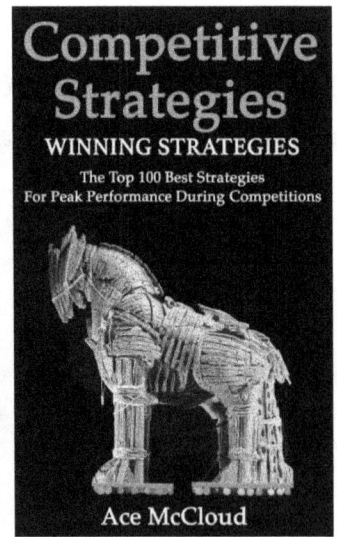

Competitive Strategies

WINNING STRATEGIES

The Top 100 Best Strategies
For Peak Performance During Competitions

Ace McCloud

Health Books

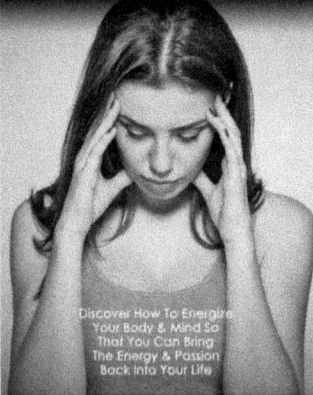

Be sure to check out my audio books as well!

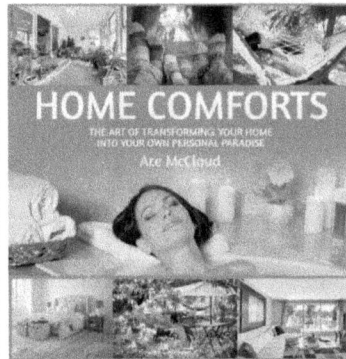

Check out my website at: **www.AcesEbooks.com** for a complete list of all of my books and high quality audio books. I enjoy bringing you the best knowledge in the world and wish you the best in using this information to make your journey through life better and more enjoyable! **Best of luck to you!**

www.ingramcontent.com/pod-product-compliance
Lightning Source LLC
Chambersburg PA
CBHW081549220326
41598CB00036B/6624